GHOST ORCHID

For Andrew,
with admiration from
a fellow Jerome
enthusiast ~
Warmly,

Maurya Simon
April 2004

ALSO BY MAURYA SIMON

The Enchanted Room

Days of Awe

Speaking in Tongues

The Golden Labyrinth

A Brief History of Punctuation

GHOST ORCHID

POEMS BY

Maurya Simon

Red Hen Press 🐔 Los Angeles

GHOST ORCHID

Cover art by Baila Goldenthal

Cover photo by Robert Falk

Cover and book design by Mark E. Cull

ISBN 1-888996-84-6
Library of Congress Catalog Card Number: 2004090112

The City of Los Angeles Cultural Affairs Department,
California Arts Council and
the Los Angeles County Arts Commission
partially support Red Hen Press.

Red Hen Press
www.redhen.org

First Edition

Printed in Canada

Acknowledgments

The author wishes to thank the editors of the following magazines and journals in which these poems originally appeared:

Agni: All Souls' Day
Alkali Flats: Lucifer in Starlight
American Literary Review: The Soloist, The Search
Caprice: Coward
Colorado Review: Season of Joy
The Georgia Review: Aphrodite Tempts God
The Gettysburg Review: The Ravens, Ode to Beelzebub
Mosaic: Unfinished Psalm (previously titled "Forty Five")
Mockingbird: Lament
Poetry International: The Fallen Angel, Doomsday
Prosodia: The Great Whiteness Unchanging
Quarterly West: Black Haloes
Runes 2002: An Unkempt Brilliance I Fear But Cannot Name
Shenandoah: Enough
Shirim: The Rapture
Smartish Pace: Banished, Invocation
The Sow's Ear Poetry Review: Angels, Lament, A Season of Virtues
The Watershed Anthology II: Benediction
Verse: Between Heaven and Earth
The Wilshire Review: God Bathing

I'm also grateful to co-editors Erin Belieu and Susan Aizenberg for including "All Souls' Day," "Doomsday," "The Search," and "Coward" in their wonderful anthology, *The Extraordinary Tide: Contemporary American Women's Poetry* (Columbia University Press, 2001).

Thanks also to Mark Jarman and David Cannady who featured "The Seven Deadly Sins," "Sacrilege," "God's Scarcity," and "Benediction" in January 2000 on PoetryNet's website.

For Alexander Jacob Flores Falk,
the newest member of the tribe

TABLE OF CONTENTS

Pale sunlight,
pale the wall.

Love moves away.
The light changes.

I need more grace
than I thought.

Rumi

I

Between Heaven and Earth

*To stay the same is to become
a diminished thing.*
Friedrich Nietzsche

*The world of dew
Is the world of dew.
And yet, and yet—*
Issa

THE RAVENS

Magisterial in pitch-blackened suits, loud envoys
From the realm of the dead, the ravens are gone.
All autumn the dusks have been cured of their cries.

Instead, the chimney smoke curls into small fists,
And blue jays, woozy with new-found dominions of air,
Flaunt their own pantomime of arrivals or departures.

Why have the ravens left town like a feathered exodus
Of the collective spirit? Conflagrations of dark flames
Singe my dreams nightly, giving shape to absence,

Yet I have seen where they have flown en masse—
Thousands gather like bats around Thunder Mountain,
Tattering its timber-line, the sky wild with wings.

And it is You they meet there, surely, for why else
Their throngs whirling, dipping, soaring like omens,
Their bodies obsidian flints striking softly against

Heaven's resonant silence, their dark-bird voices
Ancient with longing, tangled and blunt, so human?
Like Moses, I have climbed that holy mountain,

And I have watched the ravens weight vast currents
Of air with resurrected cries, but still I'm blind
To their purpose and feel alone, diminished.

And like Elijah restored to earth, I have known
Another world, but I cannot name it nor return there.
Why give to ravens what You withhold from me?

What is this drama of roaring wing-beats You ignite?
Your divinity divides the world. You are a shadow,
Massive and billowing, more secretive than death.

TRANSUBSTANTIATION

First the high road, then a bend
in the river. Soon, a crossing, the sound
of waves, and finally, a clearing:

like a dragon's mouth, Galilee glistens,
white caps for teeth; a tongue of sunlight
streaks across the fiery blue—

Here the beleaguered come: the lame,
the amputees, the fly-covered misfits;
wan pilgrims pitched onto weeping shores.

And golden is he who steps out daily
from the dark rooms of shadow—
the man whom stray dogs feverishly guard,

he who can summon the stars at noon,
who blinks throngs of wasps into flight,
who makes the dun stones speak before

they blossom into bread, who comforts
the dying, passing his fingertips over
their lips as lightly as a kiss.

And there is an arc of strangeness
about his form, as if a black swan
invisibly cradles his shoulder blades—

as if the soft machines of air
erase his breath with plumes of scent
culled from the cedars of Lebanon—

And he is as a temple before them.
No birds sing in his presence, nor dreams
visit the children humming like locusts.

There are the pangs of love suffered
even by shoals of fish the outcasts net
from the water's pastures; the scarlet

and black gifts of tongues that vultures
offer as their worship; the little live things
that women bring: all ceremonies of devotion.

The sound of quarreling waves quiets when
he passes, and the wide maw of horizon
turns fangless and silken, tamed by love.

He is no prophet, but simply a man
chosen by the lion, shaped by exile,
a measure of music traveling deserts,

a singed offering, a white sparrow,
a fugitive sorrow, a flask of spring snow,
a user's manual of the spirit—

and you will know him when he arrives
without fanfare, without hosannas,
for the face he wears is your own.

Doomsday

Slowly, like a hot tear tracing the skin's folds,
God drew His finger along my parted lips,

Then down, down along the round swelling of my chin,
Then slowly He skimmed my curved nape of neck—

Soft as a dove's throat and bare of any scent—
Turning delicately around my wingless collarbones,

His finger pulled its burning torch down to my breast
That pounded so I shook, down to my hardened aureole,

Its tiny halo enflamed, engorged with milk—
Where He hesitated only a millisecond before

Letting His finger meander further down, gravity
Lowering my eyes too, as slowly His fingertip undulated

Along the corrugation of my ribs, and down again,
Grazing now across my taut expanse of belly,

Where He paused momentarily to circle my naval softly
Before His finger moved on further down, down

To my tenderest mouth flushed with blood, blushing with
God's breath upon it, His finger rousing me there,

Stroking my trembling nether lips, rubbing them gently,
First the one, then the other, then the tiny tidal wave

That rose to meet His finger's playful, painful touch—
The aching, rising pitch of flesh turning everything to fire—

And then, all the universe—extinguished:
God took His hand away.

ALL SOULS' DAY

I ask you, Is your soul still open?
Does the sound of Gabriel's trumpet
Install in you the glory of God?

I am a weak creature: I find fault
With the universe and its creator,
Whom—or whatever—that may be—

And there are days when I'm undone
By a nameless grief, by my marrow
Singing only to itself for alms.

And there are weeks when love
Appears to me—in the form of a dog—
And I can no longer bear to call it.

So, I ask you, Where does it dwell,
This thing called soul, this mirage
I feel pricking my nerves with gall,

This clear shadow made manifest only
By doubt and doubt's sister, trouble,
Or by doubt's beleaguered bride, faith?

I have waited, like a saint, alone
On the Bridge to Nowhere, and I swear
To all that is unholy and sacred:

My soul, my perplexed spirit, keeps
Its vigil all night, awaiting a sign,
Like a ship that can never dock.

BANISHED

Who is the third who walks always beside you?
                    T.S. Eliot

We re-enter Eden in our dreams.
Riding a celestial barge, we drift back
To its shimmering waters, its frozen music.

But now our dreams of it are tarnished:
We bear the grit of the world on our palms;
A pressure of loss glosses our eyelids.

Still, we remember how the garden's air
Was once so sweet, we drank it like wine,
How like angels we moved, cowled in grace.

What was our equivalent of sleep
In that long lost sanctuary? Not death . . .
Now, grief seeps in as we trespass Eden,

As our sleep-held vision unveils terrors:
Fallen lords hang in the golden trees;
There are streaks of anger in the quartz.

And there is a going loose in fear:
Our fingers tremble as we reach to touch
Each other, as we harvest the bruised figs.

We walk Eden's perimeters like ghosts.
We want to return to the known world,
Where our mortality is still a blessing.

But the dream persists and awakens us
To the presence of a third walking always
Beside us: the shadow we can't shrug off,

Nor outrun, nor transform into truth:
The third wills itself like conscience to us—
Yet it is mute, a hovering mirage haunting

Our every word and step in and out of Eden—
And yet, believe me, it's a stranger to us,
Though we, strangers in this familiar land,

Long in its midst for some sudden glory,
For its touch upon our waking lives,
For its breath to stir in us redemption,

To save us from despair: but it is silent.
Thus, we endure our exile as God's clowns,
And the third beside us bows down to us.

GOD BATHING

Like no other, this delicate wash
Where water prisms His feet,

Where the air plays connoisseur
To His diaphanous light.

Clouds gather around His hair,
Spangling it with snowdrifts.

Nothing hugs His nakedness
But hope, and He flushes now

Because we, earth-anchored,
Bask in the clear run-off

From His cleansing, feel
Cool runnels of dew cascade

Down and consecrate us
Like pale flowers.

Like no other: this
Silent immersion.

God's Scarcity

In exile it's hard to love God.
   Christopher Buckley

Why did I await the descent of God
With an angelic ardor, armed lightly
With my soul-catcher's noose, a bridle
Made from the devil's bones, my mount
The sweet green earth that held me fast?

Why was I forever in exile from Him,
Ever the fool in an anchorite's fusty rags?
Begging the forests for signs of grace,
Wandering the chiaroscuro of leafy trails,
I cocked my ears for the rustle of robes—

Such searching led nowhere but back
To the sturdy self, to the me made servile
To the harness of flesh I wore all my days
As a mantle of thorns or a roseate shroud.
Yet I longed for a rupture in air's chrysalis,

For a portal to open wide before me, for
A shock of terror or jubilation to seize me
As on judgement day, for God to vanquish
My being with incandescence, to slide from
My bones my molecular raiment, to lift

What was left of me—oh, splendid zero!—
Heavenward, to carry me home, at last,
In a crystal thimble, a humbled essence
Of being— His most unlikely minion
Tethered only to light . . .

Between Heaven and Earth

What genius the weather shows for drama:
instead of flies, a cobweb traps diamonds,

and look how all the trees wear crystal
earrings balanced from their lobes—

even the corner bank's glazed with riches
unattainable but through the offices

of winter's sleight-of-hand flourishes,
its generosity of cold. And the river

unwinds its breath slowly like a diva dying
for having too much loved her freedom—

still, she's aglitter with oily rainbows.
The freshest beauty commences first

in the eye's cathedral, where a blueness
of sky blooms into the brain's exaltations,

where awe rises and rises in a tide
of embraces and farewells.

II

Angels of Mercy

Solitude is paradise.
Samuel Beckett

[I]n the realm of the sacred, what seems
incomplete or unattainable my be
abundance after all.
Kathleen Norris

ANGELS

Who are without mercy,
Who confide in trumpet flowers,
Who carry loose change in their pockets,
Who dress in black velvet,
Who wince and fidget like bats,
Who balance their haloes on hatracks,
Who watch reruns of famine,
Who powder their noses with pollen,
Who laugh and unleash earthquakes,
Who sidle in and out of our dreams
Like magicians, like childhood friends,
Who practice their smiles like pirates,
Who exercise by walking to Zion,
Who live on the edge of doubt,
Who cause vertigo but ease migraines,
Who weep milky tears when troubled,
Whose night sweats engender the plague,
Who pinion their arms to chandeliers,
Who speak in riddles and slant rhymes,
Who love the weak and foolhardy,
Who lust for unripe persimmons,
Who scavenge the fields for lost souls,
Who hover near lighthouses,
Who pray at railroad crossings,
Who supervise the study of rainbows,
Who cannot blush but try,
Who curl their hair with corkscrews,
Who honeymoon with Orion,
Who are not wise but pure,
Who behave with impious propriety,
Who hourly scour our faces with hope,
Whose own faces glow like radium,
Whom we've created in our own form,
Who are without mercy, seek and yearn
To return us like fossilized roses
To the wholeness of our original bloom.

BLACK HALOES

How does God hold up heaven?
We who wear His curse like a plague,
We who have fallen five hundred fathoms
Below His grace, who cringe like curs
Offered scraps by thieves—it is we
Who balance His scaffolds, who upraise
Our aching arms eternally to bear up
The golden planks and invisible girders,
Who balance huge cloudbanks on our heads,
Who hold up His gilt rafters and ceilings.

He has marked us well so none mistake us:
Though winged, we remain flightless,
Though immortal, we yearn for a reprieve,
Though comely, we're repugnant to others,
Though undamned, we exist among flames.
Black haloes are suspended above our heads:
Our rings of gold tarnished over with grit.
Our only misdemeanor: a mineral existence
Troubled by doubt, disbelief, defiance.

Still, we were good men and women.
We believed. We gave alms to the poor;
We made ourselves gardens of pure deeds.
We sang canticles of love in His name.
Now, even the vultures snicker at us
As they flap past like the devil's wind.
Was it a sin to laugh at His solemnity?
Did our misgiving habits of flesh and mind
Postpone our access to heavenly pleasures?

Why can't God hold up heaven without us?
Our haloes slip and tilt, sag like doilies.
We suffer great pangs of yearning, despite
His lofty provisions of rosy forgiveness.
Holy outcasts, chastened zeros— we hum
Our harmonium's chord, pitched high above
Limbo, but we remain grace-haunted, stilted,
Lashed like vines to the pillars of paradise:
Forever upholding this Kingdom of Sighs.

THE INNER CIRCLE

Why should we concern ourselves
With God's scarcity on earth?

Here, among us, He exists
As an abundance, faith's welter.

Yet eon after eon we observe
How mortals, prisoners of change,

Search for His hieroglyphic heart;
They serve as disciples of loss,

Rather than of daily wonder,
The yeasty stuff that fuels love.

We can't teach the mortals awe—
It must grow inside them: a crystal,

Or a spider's dew-drenched web of scrim
Spinning itself out of pure nothingness,

Or from despair, the devil's dross.
So, we devise points of arrival

And departure: we concoct small miracles,
Sudden insight, as when a gloaming sky

Transports beauty to the pulse,
When the mystery of night descends.

Our circle relishes its work:
One seraph among us busies himself

With a musical sociology of vapors;
Another moistens the movement of stars;

One provides a pulley of temperatures,
So fevered flesh may know rapture.

And some among us scrutinize desire—
That venous surge that haunts our memory—

But they're discouraged, seeing how
The world seethes like a cauldron with it—

Yet desire's as elusive as pain, as unstable
As mercury, as excessive as genius.

Better to occupy ourselves with love,
Which is manifest within every creation,

From the moth's softest articulations,
To the incandescence of fog.

Never sated, love's a sacred hunger
Replenished by awe—a milky sustenance

That unfurls like a rose's white petals
Upon which each living spirit feeds.

The Fallen Angel

One more tithe to the altar of seductions:
a rose tattoo on her rotund rump, and for that
she's lifted her dress, tucks a round of bills
into her sequined G-string, her lips pursed.
As she bends down to unfasten her garter,
the golden clump of hairs on her pubis points
its damp goatee to a breathless audience—
singed, the balding insurance salesman,
scalded, the Vietnam vet amputee wringing
his empty sleeve like it's the enemy's throat,
stricken, the barmaid who's seen it all before,
but who's in love with the star of Pussy Galore.
Haloed by cigarette smoke, the stripper moves now
as if traversing a slow dream—her blue dress
a silken sheen, a diaphanous mist thinly clinging
to her body—reptilian, sultry, she pulls her palms
and silvered fingers around her swollen breasts;
she sways to the silent baying of the hounds,
to the groundswell of heartbeats and tambourines;
she shimmies her cobalt hem waistward, and now
she ploughs her hands down until her fingertips
touch and tender that dew-spangled curl of flesh—
and she is moaning softly now, her violet eyes shut,
her chin tilted back like a flask of champagne
ready to exhale its evanescent song, her lips
swollen open, a mirror image to her flushed sex:
she is taken up in ecstasy, her spine arching back—
as if by invisible wings she's being drawn away
from the heaving men, their minds aflame, burning
like molten coils, their desire the oil-rich fuel
igniting her return to God.

ENOUGH

Heaven has enough windows for everyone,
Yet there's a secret wedged behind each pane.
God seals His lips with paraffin, but
The devil knows how to speak in tongues.

There's a secret wedged behind each pain
A mortal man or woman feels; we're dumb,
But the devil knows how to speak in tongues:
He voices our longings in wind and rain.

Each mortal man and woman feels numb
When gazing through the windows of heaven,
Where our longings are voiced in windy rain.
(Hell has no windows, only endless tunnels.)

Still gazing up to the windows of heaven,
We search for God, but He's not there.
In windowless Hell, beyond the tunnels,
We'll find him at last, burning the air.

We search for God, but He's not where
We thought we'd find Him—burning the air
In Hell's kitchen, beyond our tunnel vision.
Instead, He's gazing into our earthly windows,

Watching as flesh-bound men and women drown
In longing for that primal garden, where God
Rained down in a golden silence, and was nowhere
And everywhere at once, housed in each breast.

A Season of Virtues

I. Faith

John Gray's terrier watched over his master's grave
In Greyfriar's Kirkyard for twenty years.
Called "Bobby" by John, the dog would not budge
From that cold mound that stank of bones and love.

What does a dog know of either time or death?
No more than we, nor less. But Bobby knew
Something that amazed all Edinburgh town—
And now his secret's our drinking fountain.

II. Hope

The long chain of flowers we often refer to
As life— made of daisies, violets, and phlox—
Rose, and still rises, from a field of blood,
And loops itself over a bower of barbed wire.

Late-bloomers all, these tiny architects of Troy,
True-blue troubadours that sing in the light of day.
But the chain severs, blossoms strewn as tears;
The seeds burn like teeth in the mouths of war.

Weeds form a secular clergy. Hansel and Gretel
Knew them, gathered them for food, and survived.
Hard-bitten, scorned, some weeds choke their own;
Others masquerade as birds of passage: new chains.

And the torn rope of colors amasses the toxic:
Hemlock, datura, foxglove, & deadly nightshade—
They sustain us too, though we scorch their stems,
Though we trample them, forget their names.

Hi, Andrew! How are you? Hope all's 9-17-07
well. Thanks for lending me this book.
Sorry it took me so long to get it back
to you. I've since graduated from CSULB
with my MFA in creative writing in poetry. It
was so much work! 60 units in 2 yrs. I'm
glad I did it but also glad it's over. We've
also moved from Pasadena to Huntington Beach.
My dad sold our family home of 40 yrs.
There was a lot to so thru sh! I'll actually
be moving again soon back to Europe
mid - November. How's everything with you?
Still teaching? writing? researching, etc.?
Hope it's all going smoothly!   Love,
                                    Ellen

P.S. Did I tell you I got a hand carved Wizard staff? It's pretty cool!

This frail chain of flowers fringed with weeds
Unfurls even in December, despite the gloom.
Let us cup our hands around these tender buds,
Rosettes, umbels and sepals, as around a flame.

III. Charity

When the Bosnian boy was shot down
In the marketplace in Sarajevo, a sparrow
Alighted on his bleeding hand that still
Gripped the handlebar of his shattered bicycle.
"Don't be scared," the boy whispered to the bird.
And then he shut his eyes, dying amid awful cries.
And the sparrow flew back into this world.

IV. Justice

Why must she stand here blindfolded,
As she extends and balances her scales?

Moss has crept over her bare feet, where
Her sandals have frayed, disintegrated.

I would fill her one scale with blue scarabs
And scorpions, with short words of wisdom;

The other I would polish, so that its emptiness
Gleams heavily with the weight of sunlight.

Good and evil are equally weightless, though
Their atomic structures replicate heavy metals:

So why must dark or light fill each hollow?
Forget her scales. Rip off her blindfold!

Her heart is her amulet, her mind, gold.
Take her hand, lead her from the pedestal

As she leaves behind the bifid world—
Open-eyed, shaken, brave and unsteady...

V. Fortitude

The antlion sinks like a blessing,
(Or a curse, if you're an ant),
Down beneath a sandy corral.

Its joy is small, tucked in its legs.
Grains crowd its body into stillness.
It waits, like God, for a quiver or touch.

Its breath is a wisp of ether.
Lakes of dew poise over its head.
It is an invisible church in our midst.

VI. Prudence

Showing care and foresight,
Discretion,
The executioner explains
To the condemned man
How long it takes for the voltage
To render him unconscious,
How he must evacuate his bowels
Tonight, for decency's sake,
How his body will be treated
Afterwards.

The doomed man weeps quietly
Into his own hands,
In plain view of the executioner.
Later, when he's grown silent,
Both of them dwell—for a sustained
Moment—outside of time,
In an occasion of strange grace.
Then the executioner
Meticulously transcribes
On the Logbook of Last Words
The other man's tears.

VII. Temperance

After the Thunder Mountain fire had devoured
Thousands of acres of woodlands, for miles
Blackened the air with hot and sooty billows,
Charred into a gothic nightmare oaks, pines,
Yuccas, squirrels, lizards, and deer mice—

After the embered roots were doused, slowly
People returned to see if they'd been lucky,
If their cabins and belongings had been spared.
One man, a neighbor still wearing his slippers,
Found nothing left but a slush of ashy garnish

Littered over the ground where once had stood
The place he'd built himself forty years before,
With its ponderosa ceiling and winding stairs.
He took a long look at that steaming debris,
Shook his head, turned, rolled up his sleeves.

III

Lucifer in Starlight

The soul must lead itself to execution.
Eckhart von Hochheim

LUCIFER IN STARLIGHT

How well-lit his mind,
the turbines of his cells charged by gin.

He's a shape-shifter, an X
marking the crossroads of time and chance:

tonight, an Adonis, predator
of ethereal co-eds whose only mantra

is *perhaps, perhaps*—or else,
he's chanting Aramaic, Latin liturgies,

sweat stains scything his armpits,
his moustache glazed with powdered sugar.

He arrives unsummoned, huge
as the world's chronicles of war,

or tiny as the inchworm
drilling through Eve's apple core.

He loves us too dearly;
that's the crucible of his doubt,

the eternal torment of his days,
his raison d'être, his bittersweet conundrum.

Thus, he's doubly exiled, and
by yearning for return, he's doomed

like each of us
to dwell in an invisible house.

During the smoke-perfumed dusks,
I hear his baritone voice calling out

plaintively to all the provinces;
I see him strolling in his velour overcoat,

his violet eyes misted over
like the window-panes of cathedrals—

I reach out to test
his shameless, undisguised cheek—

fleshed over fire—
and I recoil, a wing-singed moth.

I see how human he is,
how utterly abandoned, like each of us,

to that perpetual desire
for what burns beyond speech, beyond touch.

ODE TO BEELZEBUB

Somehow you've been reduced to a hapless myth,
Yet somehow yours has been a glandular fate,

Like that of the albino angel, a helium virgin,
Who lifted off into space like a chrome rocket,

But plummeted instead into the blistering hands
Of curious strangers. Don't know that story? Well,

There are others: long tales of how your weakness
For human guile undid you, earning hollow applause.

But my tribute is sincere: I praise you, old foe,
Coal czar and bedazzling curmudgeon, passé anarchist,

And terrorist of termites—you, the poet laureate
Of latrines, of censored skeletons, damaged fruit.

If ever you wielded power, we've slowly usurped it,
And now, at the edge of the millennium, I find you

Tweaking havoc with the eyelashes of the baffled,
Hot-wiring dozing brains with armageddons of pure lust,

Or idly superimposing nuclear rainbows onto dust.
Oh, maestro of migraines, blundering architect of greed,

Surely your greatest thrills now manifest themselves
In a chronology of earth's degradations and ailments:

Massacres of bats, the demise of frogs, salamanders,
Spotted owls, white whales, and ring-tailed cats—all

Endangered creatures, bright features of His imagining—
It's a fool's sanctuary you've made of toxic fumes;

And yet, you're at home here, fingering each new doom
As if it were a nugget charm to hang (like Kali's skulls)

Upon your necklace that tightens into a golden noose.
You've still got panache. I see it in your plutonium eyes,

In the crocodile tears you weep as acid rain, even
In the cordial handshakes of the damned who wheel

And deal like crazy in the breezeways of inferno.
How can I not praise you, when you rule as primo fascist

Of the middle and lower firmaments, kingpin of sinners,
Villain of the virtuous who need your blackguard template

To redefine what is good, to relocate amoral spines?
Today I saw you lounging in a café on the boulevard,

Dressed in Armani garb, and smoking a Cuban cigar,
Sipping cappuccino instead of holy water, dining on

Vegetarian haggis and caviar with manicured hands,
Your feet propped up on a chair's velvet cushion,

Your thinning hair turned platinum—and all the while,
Lovely men and women eyeing your aquiline profile—

Yes, you still know how to live. And we to die,
Your smile lingering on our trembling lips.

THE SEVEN DEADLY SINS

The fiery,/ the fundamental God/ is mad, again.
                    Thomas Lux

I. Pride

We are betrayed by other destinations.
Let ourselves be the end-all and end-stop
Of our searching, for we come first:
We are the universal, royal, editorial *We.*
We come last, for we deserve the attention:
We are greater than He.

II. Wrath

May you waste away in the subterranean hallways
Of the Devil, where those who study the black arts
Gnaw on the tailings of your shadow for sustenance.

May your teeth turn to feathers, so that your lies
Dust the air noiselessly; your tongue become an oar,
So as to keep your breath stirred by your cries.

May the dead rise like doornails from hell's floor
To pierce your heels and soles until they bleed,
Then turn to molten tar in your veins, to adders.

May the lustful Devil visit you daily, and decide
To adopt you as his bitch, harnessing you to his bed,
So he'll hoist himself on your back & you'll be fucked.

III. Envy

Kings have long hands, Queens fine fingers.
Movie stars boast smooth faces, rare cars.

Bankers keep empty pockets and money ambassadors
Who buy them fresh loaves and discrete lovers.

Athletes enjoy steel hearts, supreme genes.
Presidents get to fly in their own jets.

Gods get immortality, great publicity.
Me, I get envy, and it makes me sick.

IV. Lust

Blood threads a fiery filigree beneath my skin.
My heart simmers, then boils like black pudding.
I want to scream, but instead I spread my knees.

It doesn't matter how many times you take me—
Entering my body like a locomotive, steaming
And hissing, your throttle open—it isn't enough.

V. Gluttony

After the turkey hen's breast and the wild rice
Stuffing, after the candied yams, green olives,
The radicchio salad with artichoke heart marinara,
After the mid-meal asparagus soup, the baguettes,
The apple compote and peach sorbet, after coffee
Liqueur and Godiva chocolates, peppermint tea and
A Gauloise cigarette, I ask you . . . What's next?

VI. Avarice

I want more of everything, the lucky one said,
More fame, more cars, more mansions, more power.

I want more vision, the bodhisattva sighed,
More insight and wisdom, more light, more distance.

I want more love, the beloved cajoled,
More sacrifice, gifts, more kisses, your soul.

I want more money, the gambler whispered,
More gold and silver, more luck, more hours.

I want more truth, the poet confessed,
More answers, more questions, and more success.

I want what I can't have, more than anything,
The miser said, more than being alive or dead.

VII. Sloth

Like a furred sling, the sloth hangs upside-
Down from the burnished branch.
His eyes are closed, all his toes curled.
He is going nowhere slowly, or else
He is going somewhere quickly, depending upon
His location in time and space, and ours.
Einstein would have looked at him just as he
Looked at stars imploding in the outer cosmos:
Going nowhere fast, or going somewhere at a snail's pace.
Why waste time doing this or that?
I'd rather know nothing about eternity or sloths.
Perhaps I'll write a poem. Perhaps not.

SWELTER

The kindest of monsters, the Devil doles out
Ice cubes today to four hijacked come-latelies:
Two mournful realtors who sold themselves,
And two war criminals with greasy smirks.

Ugly as sin, the Devil is still courteous,
Ever ready to assist with a sober rereading
Of a newcomer's decree of banishment,
A short text he translates from Aramaic.

His pack of hell-hounds shadow his steps
Like sinewy wraiths, all flame and muscle,
Snarl and famished ribs—they love him so.
Now he gives his recruits the Grand Tour,

Graciously stepping over sulphurous bubbles
Of brimstone that lead everywhere and nowhere
At once, though all paths here slant downwards.
Oh, *hell is vast, hell is capacious,* he murmurs

Softly, then a crushing smile—an ambassador
To the core—his ruby eyes radiant, devouring.
They go the usual rounds: the Bridge of Bones
To Torturers' Tower, where harpooned whalers

Dangle like bait, and ten executioners' heads
Festoon the parapets: the thermal air is briny
With tears, and heat's ferocity sears off desire;
Yet see how beneath the Adulterers' Alcove—

With its black turtledoves chuckling hotly—
Entangled couples resume mechanical fucking,
While onlookers (voyeurs) masturbate wildly,
Their palms smeared with red chili peppers.

The Devil leads his entourage to the brink
Of a glass-strewn cliff (feet trailing blood),
Where, with a long arm's flourish, he urges
Them to lean over its edge, to see how far

Below a hundred thousand writhing souls
Screech and howl in a heaving pit of lava,
The deafening din splitting their eardrums.
The four are shedding their clothing now,

Sweating from the rising heat like stuck pigs;
And the Devil tsk-tsks, nods them on without
A word to a lush, dew-lit pasture. Come sit,
He beckons, and they (quick studies) obey,

Easing their crisp, hell-weary limbs down
Onto grass (astro turf) that's hot and slick,
Their crestfallen faces emptied out of hope.
The Devil lights a thin cigarette with his tail.

Today, because I'm in a festive mood, for you
I'm breaking my God-forsaken rules: so choose
Your best-beloved torment, my doomed friends.
The smoke rings he blows form grimy haloes

Above the hell-hounds' heads: they snap at them.
The realtors begin to weep; the war criminals
Argue in an African tongue—they can't decide.
Impatient, the Devil waves aside their cries

With a graceful hand, says, I prefer the gift
Of sin-specific punishments, but I propose today,
Instead, an exchange of inflicted retributions:
You murderous two shall spend eternity selling

Prime footage property overlooking Lava Pit
To blind and deaf sadists—what purer joy?
You realtors will be cursed with sewing back
Into ruptured bodies the entrails these two

Warmongers disemboweled from their victims.
Can damned souls look aghast? Mortified?
Indeed. The Devil watches their faces harden,
Then he laughs out fireflies into the sky.

The field around them shimmers with mirages.
The hounds' fetid panting shakes the ground.
The Devil stands, bows, then raises the edges
Of his crimson cape quickly, and spins himself

Into a whirling wind of heat, a tall inferno
Gritty with graphite, blackened scales of skin.
Dazed, the four sit immobile as the hell-hounds
Howl and chase the fiery twister out of sight.

And now live flames engulf the four in a bier;
Their screams and lamentations ignite the field.
All hell's denizens pause only briefly to note how
The temperature now feels four degrees higher.

IV

The Soloist

If God lived on earth,
people would break his windows.
Yiddish proverb

If you love God, you can become holy in ten years,
if you hate Him, you can do it in two.
Anonymous

THE SOLOIST

cum grano salis

It was my turn to dance with God—
And I'd just pulled on a brash new body,

One sweet with bruises from the afterlife—
When it began to snow on our gathered tribes,

And all the angels dimmed their haloes in unison,
So darkness settled on us like a universal sin:

Oh, how God fumed then, bellowing like a bishop
Stung by the prongs of Beelzebub's fork;

He saw how His mind had unwittingly sloughed
Itself, how His memories fell like dandruff

Spiraling down from His powdery wig of cosmos.
Now it was my turn to do the impossible—

Who'd chosen me to outshine my soul?—
So I slapped God hard across His trembling thigh,

(I was small as doubt; He was larger than life),
And He wept hailstones from His cobwebbed eye.

God who is mightier than the raindrop's skirl,
Who swallows whole the world's woes,

Who cherishes none, and loves us all to death—
Dance on, dance on alone.

SEASON OF JOY

He has a hole where His heart used to be,
And it roars with time.
Perhaps He's forgotten that it's gone—
His heart buoyed off like a jellyfish.
A breeze now polishes His whalebone ribs.

The universe expands and contracts slowly
As His lungs bloom and shrink with algae.
His stomach, anxious and sated at once,
Yearns to be lost and found, a golden ducat,
But it's trapped in the belly of a lie.

His liver's being devoured by spiders;
His bladder drowns itself in Zydeco music;
His pancreas dresses up nightly as the devil.
It goes on binges, eyes the Spice Islands.
Is there no obedience school for bodily parts?

(Physician, heal thyself: grow a new heart.)
I'm not good at taking my own advice, God says,
But I'm blessed with a photographic memory.
Then he smiles. The aurora borealis pales,
Then releases the scent of wild roses.

THE SEARCH

I'm sick of celestial whodunits, wherein God
multiplies Himself like the eyes of a fly,

and blows another version of redemption
into the golden pores of the sunflower,

and inflates the tulip's mansion with ghosts.
Rubied maple leaves bloody the ground

with tattered clues to the afterlife;
acorns concern themselves, like plump nuns,

with the sacraments of summer that worms
sequester as holy grails. I have lost my way.

I'm weary of the world of deeds and men—
oh world of ten thousand leavings and losses.

The Great Sleuth of meaning divides Himself
too thinly for comfort and dwells alone

in this patchwork universe, surveying our sins
of omission, the falling stars His hot tears—

and love's the only grace binding us
to each other with invisible threads.

Where does my wandering take me, but
down into the deepest pit of bewilderment,

where my own death stares back at me,
unadorned, unforgiven, unknown?

The only mystery that counts is the one
I cannot solve. Such is my burden, my hope.

The Rapture

There is a kind of celestial music
That crushes the heart rather than
Raising it aloft in buoyant prayer.
Its melody is so drunk and swollen
By bittersweet rapture that the heart
Becomes engorged and finally bursts.
Thus saints die from such a surfeit
Of divine psalmody, their hearts
Finally knuckling under the blazing
Of His tightly clenched fist.

Aphrodite Tempts God

The round-abouts of her body made
devils even out of dead trees. -Fabian Carballo

Her thighs: a solid, marble-smooth ambrosia
that turns men of the cloth into butter—

Her calves: curved by strong muscles,
fragrant as winter hyacinth;
they segue like love letters into

Her ankles: a narrow script for movement,
a lovely lightness that tapers down into—

Her feet: lilies of the field—

Her hips: monuments to ripeness—

Her sex: enlightenment, or else a fountain
of morning dew, where lost souls wander
through eternity, yet are made anew—

Her waist: the hornet's envy,
the whalebone stay's pride and joy—

Her ribs: each one a bonus for the breath,
a chalice for aortic echoes, each nipple cochineal,
redolent of cinnamon—

Her neck: softer and sweeter than,
more graceful than the brush of a dragonfly's
shadow against the wind's cheek—

Her face: God's mirror, His dream:
a valley of damask roses,
yin curved to His yang, His sole talisman—

Her love: a wisp of nothingness . . .

COWARD

If God had a wife, she'd be a doozy,
A siren tart with luscious hips and bee-stung lips,
A master blackmailer, pedophile, Ms. Universal
Misdemeanor whose toxic bones ooze ambrosia—
A mercenary of transubstantiations,
A barefoot confection, Countess Miracula—

If God had an aunt, or a sister, a pal,
Or a grandmother, daughter, or a winsome niece,
She'd bash in the brains of all those men
God favors, then drink their blood sweetly
From a glass slipper, before calmly bowing
The cello wedged between her sultry knees—

If God had a girlfriend, a novia, a squeeze,
She'd be a monstrously pretty killer,
A slayer of archangels and liars, of mayors
And virgins and libertines—Bam! They're dead!
If God had, if only God had her, his soul mate,
His extension ladder, His only friend.

SACRILEGE

If God is love, then who are you, Mister,
With your sagging biceps and blank palms,
With your tooth-aching vengeance and third eye
Poised like a laser gun, all ready to zap dead
The hapless (or hatless), the unsaved masses?

Oh poseur, charlatan, chameleon, and chimera
Dressed in the colors of awe, striptease artist,
Shim-sham in drag, shape-shifting braggart:
Are you a transmogrifying transplant from Oz?
If God is love, then why the armor, the spears?

I'd rather be dazzled by razzamatazz sweetness
And light, be blinded by a hot blast of mercy,
Than basted by your mustard-gas breath and lies.
I'd rather be manhandled daily by demons than
Withstand your polar touch, your cruel pity.

If God is love, then yours, Mister, is twisted
Into something monstrously heavy—a slavery
Of sighs, a paucity of spirit, the dementia
Forged from suffering, a locomotion of fears—
For your love betrays the world you devised.

INVOCATION

O God—who art dust mote and fern spore,
salt crystal and dog-star, who art refinery smoke,
cumulus, leaf-rot, dishwater and spindrift—

how can I know thy invisible movements
through this world, when thou inhabit even
the debris of lives, the perforations of years?

God, who wears the green mask of death,
who visits the world in wisps of prayer,
how can I divine thy face through my tears?

Give me some sign—a thumbprint, a fragrance
of hyacinth, stigmata of coal on my brow—
that I may steep my silence in faith;

show me thy secret handshake welcoming
the weeds, thy luminous smile, thy mind
that spins the world wildly on its axis—

consecrate me as thou would the tiger's yawn,
offering itself like the poor man's bowl,
to the terrified fawn, to the wayward dove—

and I will do thy bidding, polishing words
so they gleam like ice, abandoning my rage
to kneel before thee, swallowing my doubt.

But there is no answer when I call out,
and my longing darkens my throat, my mouth.
How can I lift my eyes to a gutted sky?

O God, who art neither father nor son, nor
holy ghost, who art haloed by radium clouds,
beloved by millions of sparkplugs and ants,

thou who nestles in war's lap, in the breasts
of desire, who conspires with the darkest joys,
who art as amorphous as a map of stillness—

I cry out to thee again and again, over
and over, and only the wilderness answers,
and the dangerous world's laughter—

V

Unfinished Psalms

My God is a spiral
without beginning or end.
Walter Anderson

UNFINISHED PSALM

I like how the days crescendo into night,
the dark itself a rosary of hours,
and the full moon the soul's white pendant.

Each dawn's an anthem for someone's deliverance—
not mine—for I am still anchored to longing
like a nautilus to its spiraling house,

and only the tides of desire unloosen my hold.
December. The year dies anew, and yet
high clouds bear witness to change as they drift

into each other, reforming themselves sweetly
into origami cranes, rabbits, and doves.
Night's sum of shadows exacts my dues, but

whom to pay? The darkness offers only this
temporary, shallow solace—a quiet place—
and it says, Who are you, oh voiceless one?

The Great Whiteness Unchanging

springs from the black darkness of God,
breathes a stirring among embers and water,
unfurls from the lips of souls lost in ellipses,
suspends itself mid-air as a ghost orchid—

O most holy of zeroes and mysterious thunder,
this great whiteness unchanging, everlasting,
is a worship of stillness buried in petals:
an incarnation of dawn, parable of the rose—

it trembles in the ache of the real,
reflects itself in the lyricism of mirrors,
transcends sudden zeal and bitter longings,
it gathers beyond the sweet tyranny of sighs—

this great whiteness unchanging blurs the edges
of thought in a spirit surge: electric, transparent:
it rises as a lonely fountain of baffled ether;
it forms an empty-handed angel of air—

O holy, most holy piston of locomotion,
of stasis balanced on the lacunae of ozone,
O wicked blessing of nothingness and abundance
that cauterizes the will, breeds an awkward grace—

enter me as an invisible splinter enters flesh,
as a siren sears the eardrum, amputating thought,
as sperm penetrate the womb's ripe antechamber,
as rapture divines itself from rapture—

O great vastness unchanging, forever alive,
surpass my almanac's passion, my year's grief,
roam the firmament ready to blister my heart—
O enter me, most holy of wind-thinned flames—

fly into my throat's chariot and burn to vapor,
seep into my veins, a slow fix of molten awe,
a radiant disease: engulf my nakedness, my being,
my soul raging into an uroboros of light—

LAMENT

If poems are prayers,   then pity mine
That are hollow, heartsick,   halved by lack
Of ardor, autistic,   armless as worms,
Benighted, bereft   of buoyant faith,
Wishful and wordy,   willful, perplexed.
I seek no savior,   no sudden elation,
Nor entry to ease,   no eye of eternity.
I know the noise   of the knowable world,
And what waits whitely   beyond this world,
Are phantasms full   of filigreed dew—
That the house of hosts,   of a heavenly God,
Nests its nimbus,   its nave and temple,
Within me, invisible,   installed with countless
Exits and entrances,   each doorless.
At best, I beckon   like a bad ventriloquist
For yearning, yet   I yield to mimic
The heart's harangues,   the hard accidents
Of fate and fury,   the fool's blessings.
My mouth is mothy,   muffled by two
Soft petals, by pleas;   my pearled teeth
Are thorns that thrive   in a thicket of longings;
My tongue is torn   and tarred, is forked.
My worship is wordless: it's the wide silence
Hooding my halting,   hovering voice,
Spreading its scalding   seepage of dazzle
To bleed brightly,   like a bonfire, between
These lines and lyrics,   to light and scour
My mind's margins,   and my meanderings.
This silence simmers   and surges before
And after all thought,   answering me
Mutely, magically,   like a mad lover—
This silence my sole,   and soul's, prayer,
Sprawls beside me,   singing noiselessly
The perfect parlance   of the parenting dark.

An Unkempt Brilliance I Fear But Cannot Name

The darkness round us is deep.
  William Stafford

I cannot curse God any longer—
My tears, the tiny apostrophes of loss,
Splash onto silence, evaporate at last.

Is eternity a trove that harbors
Only the mystery of our days,
Without the torment of our nights?

I will try to speak softly, wrapped
In my chains, my voice a current
Of praise spangled with awe's pollen.

Why does the soul root itself in air?
How does it climb out from spiraling stairs
Of iridescent stars constellating the brain?

Happiness is both precarious and ancient.
Like Solomon, I sit on a makeshift throne
That wobbles when I lean toward one extreme.

And why shouldn't the soul be incestuous,
Loving sister and brother, mother and father,
Without the harnesses of guilt, remorse, shame?

God, both pistil and stamen, beckons to me,
Honey-suckler that I am: but when I slip
My tongue into irises, tulips, I sip only air.

The body, blood and muscle, muddles the mind.
The mind, fisted around ideas, bristles the soul.
Does the soul half-remember these coils?

After a death, my forebears sat shiva:
On small wooden stools they fasted, prayed.
Did God finger their cheeks with tenderness?

Yes, life's mosaic is clarified by dust,
The way a handkerchief covering a corpse's face
Blanks out the tragic jowls, the obstinate stare.

If I curse now, let me grit my teeth
Over my exile from sanctity, which,
Like alum turns the tongue fugitive.

The body can only take so much rapture.
The throaty fugues of pleasure dwindle,
Surely, to a final grace note of molecule.

Dampness settles in my heart and art—
The wash of memory blurring my questions.
There are no hard edges to the Unknown.

I think the soul must be God's template,
Or templet ("miniature temple"), that place,
Like the stanza, encompassing strange music.

How have I slipped so easily from blame
To reverence, from hurling stray stones,
To blessing my wounds, startling as garnets?

Does the soul grow in increments of grace?
Does it move from one body to the next,
Receiving a rent of purest light from each?

I am still a child dressed in wonder.
But I am naked, too, under a nightgown
Of clouds, under the shroud of my name.

Is the clatter of bones God's tambourine?
No, no— it can't be that a human thing
Yields music to ghosts— or can it?

Slight are my vows, cool my promises;
My unspent devotions are slippery as eels:
There is an unkempt brilliance I fear.

If love is eternal, then why not desire?
Its fire also pulverizes and scours,
Purifies—but perhaps that's a trick of light.

I still think that beauty is a blueprint
Of the sacred. So, why not pain, why not
The broken mouth, and the hate it spews?

Why shouldn't the soul shake itself
Free of us, like a dog exiting water?
Our mortal smell, alone, must make it gasp.

But I feel something clinging to my flesh,
Burnishing it in slow degrees like a patina
Or a rash: the touch of God-knows-what.

Is the undertow of an echo a random shifting
Of a spirit's breath, or is it merely wind
Chimed and slimmed by flight from paradise?

I'm done with curses, done with clotted anger,
Though they've led me, a churchless penitent,
To this threshold of God-hobbled astonishment.

THE AFTERLIFE

Like a hover-craft heavily straining against
Gravity, rising above choppy waves and spray,
Tipping this way and that as it struggles to level
Itself on spumes of startled air, so my soul

Floats upward from the swirl of sheets,
From the fumes of sleep-drenched flesh,
And rises mightily to poise and right itself
Above the dream-fray of my earthly body.

Its passenger, in thought-balloons, cries:
"Stop! I'm dizzy, I'm afraid," but it sails on
And upward toward the ceiling, light-hearted,
A defiant dirigible, unstartled and sublime—

My soul meanders through the room, then glides
Unbidden through the walls into the carousel
Of night, joining vast tides of turning lights.
How easy it is to say good-bye now to what

Once was firm and dear, to that word forever,
To the slumbering, land-locked urges I wore
Like negligees, to green webs and arctic silence.
There's no progress here, no weather to defy,

No nature, nor gods or devils, no history, no
Science: only the yes to a wealth of nothingness,
To golden storehouses of unknowing, and (perhaps)
To something large and looming, calling me back.

BENEDICTION

Bless the man with the torturer's mouth,
bless the woman with the fossil soul,

bless the man with the storm in his groin,
bless the woman whom no one loves,

bless the man with a skull made of iron,
bless the woman who dreams of great kingdoms,

bless the man who's strange and swift to anger,
bless the woman whose habit is silence,

bless the man who surrenders nothing,
bless the woman who's a martyr to pigeons,

bless the man who lurks in the tower,
bless the woman of no conscience, no armor,

bless the man who nightly cries "Wolf,"
bless the woman who blushes and stutters,

bless the man who subdues the trees,
bless the woman who curses the rainbow,

bless the man who is a slave to pity,
bless the woman who delights in nakedness,

bless the man who is broken by love,
bless the woman who heals herself in greed,

bless the man whose grip is slipping,
bless the woman who is dangerous with pride,

bless the man on the threshold of jumping,
bless the woman newly born into pain,

bless the man be he murderer or thief,
bless the woman drooling in her cup,

The *ghost orchid* (Polyradicon lindeni) "is a beautiful and curiously leafless epiphyte that lives in Fakahatchee Strand and a few other swamps in south Florida. Donovan Correll (1950), a noted orchid biologist, described the flower as a 'snow-white frog suspended in mid-air.'" From *Swamp Song*, by Ron Larson (University Press of Florida, 1995), page 66.

Pages 30-31: "The Inner Circle" – I owe some of the ideas fuelling this poem indirectly to a lecture, entitled "The Wisdom of Leopold Kohr," delivered by Ivan Illich and Matthias Rieger at Pitzer College in 1996.

Page 34: "A Season of Virtues" – In addition to a bronze statue of "Bobby," placed in Edinburgh's Grayfriar's Kirkyard, there's also a drinking fountain erected nearby to commemorate the dog's obstinate loyalty.

Page 36: "A Season of Virtues" –The larvae of antlions (Family Myrmeleontidae) dig funnel shaped pits under which they bury themselves to lie in wait for their prey. "Antlions are also called 'doodle bugs.' Country children of earlier generations knew that one can entice the larva to leave its pit by pronouncing the magic phrase, 'Doodle bug, doodle bug, come out of your hole.' Actually, the expirations that accompany these words . . . spoken very close to the pit, dislodge some sand, and the doodle bug—believing it has made a capture— becomes excited and crawls into view." From *Insects of the Greater Los Angeles Basin*, by Charles L. Hogue (Natural History Museum of Los Angeles County, 1993), page 148.

Page 37: "A Season of Virtues" – Before the Grand Prix wildfire, the 1980 Thunder Mt. fire was the worst wildfire in recorded history in the San Gabriel Mountains in southern California. It was started by workers burning out tree stumps, to make a new ski run, during Santa Ana wind conditions.

Page 66: "The Great Whiteness Unchanging" – This phrase derives from an essay by Samuel Beckett.

Page 73: "Benediction" is for Allen Ginsberg, in memoriam, April 5, 1997.

I owe a great debt to the following astute readers, they of great patience and even greater faith, who advised me on earlier versions of these poems: Cynthia Tuell, Nancy Ware, Frances McConnel, Wendy Herbert, Gina Meister, Doug Anderson, Judy Kronenfeld, Barbara Goldberg, Peggy Shumaker, Robert Falk, and, especially, Jack Miles who brought to his reading of this book both his considerable biblical erudition and his uncanny poetic sensibility, *deo favente*.

About the Author

Maurya Simon is the author of *The Enchanted Room* and *Days of Awe* (Copper Canyon Press, 1986, 1989), *Speaking in Tongues* (Gibbs Smith, 1990), *The Golden Labyrinth* (University of Missouri Press, 1995) and *A Brief History of Punctuation* (Sutton Hoo Press, 2002). Simon is the recipient of a 2002 Visiting Artist Residency from the American Academy in Rome, a 1999-2000 NEA Fellowship in poetry, a University Award from the Academy of American Poets, the Celia B. Wagner and Lucille Medwick Memorial Awards from the Poetry Society of America, and a Fulbright Indo-American Fellowship. She teaches in the Creative Writing Department at the University of California, Riverside and lives in the Angeles National Forest of the San Gabriel Mountains, in southern California.